Prayerful WARRIOR MOM

Medical & Prayer Journal

Prayerful WARRIOR MOM

Medical & Prayer Journal

Bringing Order to Healthcare
While Finding Peace in Prayer

TRACY A. RIPLEY

PUBLISHED BY PRAYERFUL WARRIOR LLC
www.prayerfulwarrior.com

The resources in this book are provided for informational purposes only and should not be used to replace the specialized training and professional judgment of a health care or mental health care professional.

Neither the author nor the publisher can be held responsible for the use of the information provided within this book. Please always consult a trained professional before making any decision regarding treatment of yourself or others.

Library of Congress Control Number: 2025922061
ISBN: 979-8-9932406-0-2 paperback
ISBN: 979-8-9932406-1-9 spiral bound

Printed in the United States of America

Dedicated to every caregiver walking through hospital halls and holding on to hope

Table of Contents

Introduction 1

How to Use this Journal 2

Physician Contact Information 6

Medical & Prayer Journals 10

Medical Tracker 115

Thank you! 121

Other Titles by the Author 122

From the Author

Dear Reader,

Do you find yourself asking these questions?

- *When did those symptoms first appear?*
- *What was that question I wanted to ask the doctor?*
- *When was that medicine discontinued? When did it begin?*
- *What was the date of my child or my loved one's last major surgery?*
- *How many weeks did they mention there would be restrictions?*

If you've asked any or all of these questions, this medical journal is ***designed for you***! I have been in the same boat -- wishing I had a convenient way to track this critical information.

My youngest son was born in 2013 and diagnosed fourteen hours later with a congenital heart disease (CHD). During that time, my husband and I had to divide our efforts, ensuring someone was with our infant son, while the other was home with our preschooler. As I spent countless hours, days, and weeks sitting in doctors' offices, patient waiting areas, and hospital rooms, it was important to keep my husband informed about the day's events, issues we faced, or any adverse effects that emerged. I found journaling was the most effective way to keep everything organized. In the moments, when I felt alone or worried about my son's future, I turned to God in prayer; often writing my prayers in my journal and laying my burdens at the foot of the Cross.

After struggling to find the right journal to meet my needs, I decided to create one! I hope you find it to be a valuable tool and an outlet to pour out your worries, fears, and anxiety to the Lord. He is your comforter, redeemer, and saving grace. When you lay your burdens at His feet, He hears your prayers. Ask in accordance with His Word and He will answer. For as it says in Luke 11:9:

"So I say to you, ask, and it will be given to you;
seek, and you will find;
knock, and it will be opened to you."

With love and encouragement,

Tracy A Ripley

How to Utilize this Medical Journal

This journal is meant to be flexible.

- Use it for weekly tracking to gauge changes in activity week to week or
- Use it to record only when you have an upcoming appointment or
- To document an unscheduled urgent care visit to discuss with your family doctor or specialist at your next visit

Date:

Prayerful Warrior

The first half of the medical journal is a place to keep track of concerns and questions leading up to doctor appointments or hospital visits

- Keeping track of when symptoms started, the frequency and intensity can be very helpful to your medical team
- Writing your questions down in advance of the appointment help get those important questions answered and avoid forgetting to ask them!

Change in Activity / Symptoms:

Concerns / Questions:

How to Utilize this Medical Journal

The second half of the medical journal is to document the doctor visit or hospital stay and follow up instructions

- Check the applicable boxes below based on the result of the visit
- Note any new medicine or changes to existing meds in the box provided
- The remaining boxes are to be used to describe going home instructions, limitations, and to document any lessons learned to avoid issues for next time
    - ***Be sure to note any issues that came up during the stay including adverse effects with medicine, hospital staff, or things that helped***
- ***Things to Watch*** is given its own category because this can be a ***critical point*** to ensure we are *proactive* in our medical care
    - Catching things before they escalate can be the difference between life or death in some medical cases

Medical Visit

☐ Follow up Required ☐ Hospital Stay Required ☐ Medication

New

Changed ☐ Removed ☐

Care Plans / Restrictions:

Problems / Adverse Effects:

Things to Watch / Special Instructions:

How to Utilize the Prayer Journal & Medical Tracker

- *God can handle it!*
  - ***"His yoke is easy and His burden is light" Matthew 11:30***

- *Write God a letter.*
  - *He knows what is on your heart but writing it out can help* ***release the pain, anger, or fear you are feeling.***

- ***Ask for Forgiveness in Jesus Name!***
  - *Break free from the shackles of shame, guilt, & unforgiveness that are keeping you from living the life God has planned for you!*

Lay Your Burdens at the Cross

Father in Heaven ...

Prayerful Warrior

- *The medical tracker at the back of this journal is a convenient way to keep track of hospital stays, surgeries, and major medical procedures in one convenient place!*

Physician:	EXAMPLE DOCTOR NAME	*Date:*	Jan 3-5, 2025
Location/Facility:	ABC Hospital		
Treatment:	Tympanoplasty - Right Ear		
Important Notes:	Placed under limited restrictions - Dr note provided for school		

Physician Contact Information

Physician Name: ☐ *Primary Care Physician*

Address:

Phone:

Email Address:

Website:

Physician Name: *Specialty:*

Address:

Phone:

Email Address:

Website:

Physician Name: *Specialty:*

Address:

Phone:

Email Address:

Website:

Physician Name: *Specialty:*

Address:

Phone:

Email Address:

Website:

Physician Contact Information

Physician Name: *Specialty:*

Address:

Phone:

Email Address:

Website:

Physician Name: *Specialty:*

Address:

Phone:

Email Address:

Website:

Physician Name: *Specialty:*

Address:

Phone:

Email Address:

Website:

Physician Name: *Specialty:*

Address:

Phone:

Email Address:

Website:

Physician Contact Information

Physician Name: ☐ *Primary Care Physician*

Address:

Phone:

Email Address:

Website:

Physician Name: *Specialty:*

Address:

Phone:

Email Address:

Website:

Physician Name: *Specialty:*

Address:

Phone:

Email Address:

Website:

Physician Name: *Specialty:*

Address:

Phone:

Email Address:

Website:

Physician Contact Information

Physician Name: *Specialty:*

Address:

Phone:

Email Address:

Website:

Physician Name: *Specialty:*

Address:

Phone:

Email Address:

Website:

Physician Name: *Specialty:*

Address:

Phone:

Email Address:

Website:

Physician Name: *Specialty:*

Address:

Phone:

Email Address:

Website:

Medical Journal

Change in Activity / Symptoms:

Date:

Concerns / Questions:

Medical Visit

Prayerful Warrior

☐ Medication

☐ Follow up Required

☐ Hospital Stay Required

New

Changed ☐ Removed ☐

Care Plans / Restrictions:

Problems / Adverse Effects:

Things to Watch / Special Instructions:

Prayer Journal

Lay Your Burdens at the Cross

Father in Heaven ...

"Come to Me, all you who labor and are heavy laden,
and I will give you rest."
~ Matthew 11:28

Medical Journal

Change in Activity / Symptoms:

Date:

Concerns / Questions:

Medical Visit

Prayerful Warrior

☐ Medication

☐ Follow up Required

☐ Hospital Stay Required

New	
Changed ☐	Removed ☐

Care Plans / Restrictions:

Problems / Adverse Effects:

Things to Watch / Special Instructions:

Prayer Journal

Lay Your Burdens at the Cross

Father in Heaven ...

Trust in the LORD with all your heart, And lean not on your own understanding, In all your ways acknowledge Him, And He shall direct your paths.

~ Proverbs 3:5-6

Medical Journal

Date:

Change in Activity / Symptoms:

Concerns / Questions:

Medical Visit

Prayerful Warrior

☐ Medication

New	
Changed ☐	Removed ☐

☐ Follow up Required

☐ Hospital Stay Required

Care Plans / Restrictions:

Problems / Adverse Effects:

Things to Watch / Special Instructions:

Prayer Journal

Lay Your Burdens at the Cross

Father in Heaven ...

Be anxious for nothing, but in everything by prayer and supplication, with thanksgiving, let your requests be made known to God,

~ Philippians 4:6

Medical Journal

Date:

Change in Activity / Symptoms:

Concerns / Questions:

Medical Visit

Prayerful Warrior

☐ Medication

New

Changed ☐ Removed ☐

☐ Follow up Required ☐ Hospital Stay Required

Care Plans / Restrictions:

Problems / Adverse Effects:

Things to Watch / Special Instructions:

Prayer Journal

Lay Your Burdens at the Cross

Father in Heaven ...

Your word is a lamp to my feet

And a light to my path.

~ Psalm 119:105

Medical Journal

Date:

Change in Activity / Symptoms:

Concerns / Questions:

Medical Visit

Prayerful Warrior

☐ Medication

New	
Changed ☐	Removed ☐

☐ Follow up Required ☐ Hospital Stay Required

Care Plans / Restrictions:

Problems / Adverse Effects:

Things to Watch / Special Instructions:

Prayer Journal

Lay Your Burdens at the Cross

Father in Heaven ...

And the LORD, He is the One who goes before you. He will be with you,
He will not leave you nor forsake you, do not fear nor be dismayed.

~ Deuteronomy 31:8

Medical Journal

Date:

Change in Activity / Symptoms:

Concerns / Questions:

Medical Visit

Prayerful Warrior

☐ Follow up Required

☐ Hospital Stay Required

☐ Medication

New

Changed ☐ Removed ☐

Care Plans / Restrictions:

Problems / Adverse Effects:

Things to Watch / Special Instructions:

Prayer Journal

Lay Your Burdens at the Cross

Father in Heaven ...

For He shall give His angels charge over you,
To keep you in all your ways.
~ Psalm 91:11

Medical Journal

Change in Activity / Symptoms:

Date:

Concerns / Questions:

Medical Visit

Prayerful Warrior

☐ Follow up Required

☐ Hospital Stay Required

☐ Medication

New

Changed ☐ Removed ☐

Care Plans / Restrictions:

Problems / Adverse Effects:

Things to Watch / Special Instructions:

Prayer Journal

Lay Your Burdens at the Cross

Father in Heaven ...

In the world you will have tribulation, but be of good cheer,
I have overcome the world.
~ John 16:33b

Medical Journal

Date:

Change in Activity / Symptoms:

Concerns / Questions:

Medical Visit

Prayerful Warrior

☐ Follow up Required

☐ Hospital Stay Required

☐ Medication

New

Changed ☐ Removed ☐

Care Plans / Restrictions:

Problems / Adverse Effects:

Things to Watch / Special Instructions:

Prayer Journal

Lay Your Burdens at the Cross

Father in Heaven ...

For He Himself has said,
"I will never leave you nor forsake you."
~ Hebrews 13:5b

Medical Journal

Date:

Change in Activity / Symptoms:

Concerns / Questions:

Medical Visit

Prayerful Warrior

☐ Follow up Required

☐ Hospital Stay Required

☐ Medication

New

Changed ☐ Removed ☐

Care Plans / Restrictions:

Problems / Adverse Effects:

Things to Watch / Special Instructions:

Prayer Journal

Lay Your Burdens at the Cross

Father in Heaven ...

So do not worry about tomorrow, for tomorrow will worry about itself.
Each day has enough trouble of its own.
~ Matthew 6:34 NASB

Medical Journal

Date:

Change in Activity / Symptoms:

Concerns / Questions:

Medical Visit

Prayerful Warrior

☐ Medication

New	
Changed ☐	Removed ☐

☐ Follow up Required

☐ Hospital Stay Required

Care Plans / Restrictions:

Problems / Adverse Effects:

Things to Watch / Special Instructions:

Prayer Journal

Lay Your Burdens at the Cross

Father in Heaven ...

Fear not, for I am with you, Be not dismayed, for I am your God.
I will strengthen you, Yes, I will help you,
I will uphold you with My righteous right hand.
~ Isaiah 41:10

Medical Journal

Date:

Change in Activity / Symptoms:

Concerns / Questions:

Medical Visit

Prayerful Warrior

☐ Follow up Required

☐ Hospital Stay Required

☐ Medication

New

Changed ☐ Removed ☐

Care Plans / Restrictions:

Problems / Adverse Effects:

Things to Watch / Special Instructions:

Prayer Journal

Lay Your Burdens at the Cross

Father in Heaven ...

So I say to you, ask, and it will be given to you, seek,
and you will find, knock, and it will be opened to you.
~ Luke 11:9

Medical Journal

Date:

Change in Activity / Symptoms:

Concerns / Questions:

Medical Visit

Prayerful Warrior

☐ Follow up Required ☐ Hospital Stay Required ☐ Medication

New

Changed ☐ Removed ☐

Care Plans / Restrictions:

Problems / Adverse Effects:

Things to Watch / Special Instructions:

Prayer Journal

Lay Your Burdens at the Cross

Father in Heaven ...

When you pass through the waters, I will be with you,
And through the rivers, they shall not overflow you.
When you walk through the fire, you shall not be burned,
Nor shall the flame scorch you.

~ Isaiah 43:2

Medical Journal

Date:

Change in Activity / Symptoms:

Concerns / Questions:

Medical Visit

Prayerful Warrior

☐ Follow up Required

☐ Hospital Stay Required

☐ Medication

New

Changed ☐ Removed ☐

Care Plans / Restrictions:

Problems / Adverse Effects:

Things to Watch / Special Instructions:

Prayer Journal

Lay Your Burdens at the Cross

Father in Heaven ...

God is our refuge and strength,
A very present help in trouble.
Therefore we will not fear,
~ Psalm 46:1-2

Medical Journal

Date:

Change in Activity / Symptoms:

Concerns / Questions:

Medical Visit

Prayerful Warrior

☐ Follow up Required

☐ Hospital Stay Required

☐ Medication

New

Changed ☐ Removed ☐

Care Plans / Restrictions:

Problems / Adverse Effects:

Things to Watch / Special Instructions:

Prayer Journal

Lay Your Burdens at the Cross

Father in Heaven ...

Yea, though I walk through the valley of the shadow of death,
I will fear no evil, For You are with me,
Your rod and Your staff, they comfort me.
~ Psalm 23:4

Medical Journal

Date:

Change in Activity / Symptoms:

Concerns / Questions:

Medical Visit

Prayerful Warrior

☐ Follow up Required

☐ Hospital Stay Required

☐ Medication

New

Changed ☐ Removed ☐

Care Plans / Restrictions:

Problems / Adverse Effects:

Things to Watch / Special Instructions:

Prayer Journal

Lay Your Burdens at the Cross

Father in Heaven ...

Surely goodness and mercy shall follow me
All the days of my life,
And I will dwell in the house of the LORD, Forever.
~ Psalm 23:6

Medical Journal

Date:

Change in Activity / Symptoms:

Concerns / Questions:

Medical Visit

Prayerful Warrior

☐ Follow up Required

☐ Hospital Stay Required

☐ Medication

New

Changed ☐ Removed ☐

Care Plans / Restrictions:

Problems / Adverse Effects:

Things to Watch / Special Instructions:

Prayer Journal

Lay Your Burdens at the Cross

Father in Heaven ...

'For I know the plans that I have for you,' declares the LORD,
'plans for prosperity and not for disaster,
to give you a future and a hope.'
~ Jeremiah 29:11 NASB

Medical Journal

Date:

Change in Activity / Symptoms:

Concerns / Questions:

Medical Visit

Prayerful Warrior

☐ Follow up Required ☐ Hospital Stay Required

☐ Medication

New

Changed ☐ Removed ☐

Care Plans / Restrictions:

Problems / Adverse Effects:

Things to Watch / Special Instructions:

Prayer Journal

Lay Your Burdens at the Cross

Father in Heaven ...

"My grace is sufficient for you,
for My strength is made perfect in weakness."
~ 2 Corinthians 12:9

Medical Journal

Change in Activity / Symptoms:

Date:

Concerns / Questions:

Medical Visit

Prayerful Warrior

- [ ] Medication

New	
Changed ☐	Removed ☐

- [ ] Follow up Required
- [ ] Hospital Stay Required

Care Plans / Restrictions:

Problems / Adverse Effects:

Things to Watch / Special Instructions:

Prayer Journal

Lay Your Burdens at the Cross

Father in Heaven ...

And the prayer of faith will save the sick,
and the Lord will raise him up.
~ James 5:15

Medical Journal

Date:

Change in Activity / Symptoms:

Concerns / Questions:

Medical Visit

Prayerful Warrior

☐ Follow up Required

☐ Hospital Stay Required

☐ Medication

New

Changed ☐ Removed ☐

Care Plans / Restrictions:

Problems / Adverse Effects:

Things to Watch / Special Instructions:

Prayer Journal

Lay Your Burdens at the Cross

Father in Heaven ...

But Jesus looked at them and said to them, "With men this is impossible, but with God all things are possible."

~ Matthew 19:26

Medical Journal

Date:

Change in Activity / Symptoms:

Concerns / Questions:

Medical Visit

Prayerful Warrior

☐ Follow up Required

☐ Hospital Stay Required

☐ Medication

New

Changed ☐ Removed ☐

Care Plans / Restrictions:

Problems / Adverse Effects:

Things to Watch / Special Instructions:

Prayer Journal

Lay Your Burdens at the Cross

Father in Heaven ...

Beloved, I pray that you may prosper in all things
and be in health, just as your soul prospers.
~ 3 John 1:2

Medical Journal

Date:

Change in Activity / Symptoms:

Concerns / Questions:

Medical Visit

Prayerful Warrior

☐ Follow up Required

☐ Hospital Stay Required

☐ Medication

New

Changed ☐ Removed ☐

Care Plans / Restrictions:

Problems / Adverse Effects:

Things to Watch / Special Instructions:

Prayer Journal

Lay Your Burdens at the Cross

Father in Heaven ...

He was wounded for our transgressions,
He was bruised for our iniquities,
And by His stripes we are healed.
~ Isaiah 53:5

Medical Journal

Change in Activity / Symptoms:

Date:

Concerns / Questions:

Medical Visit

Prayerful Warrior

☐ Medication

☐ Follow up Required

☐ Hospital Stay Required

New

Changed ☐ Removed ☐

Care Plans / Restrictions:

Problems / Adverse Effects:

Things to Watch / Special Instructions:

Prayer Journal

Lay Your Burdens at the Cross

Father in Heaven ...

Be still, and know that I am God,
I will be exalted among the nations,
I will be exalted in the earth!
~ Psalm 46:10

Medical Journal

Change in Activity / Symptoms:

Date:

Concerns / Questions:

Medical Visit

Prayerful Warrior

☐ Follow up Required

☐ Hospital Stay Required

☐ Medication

New	
Changed ☐	Removed ☐

Care Plans / Restrictions:

Problems / Adverse Effects:

Things to Watch / Special Instructions:

Prayer Journal

Lay Your Burdens at the Cross

Father in Heaven ...

My help comes from the LORD
Who made heaven and earth.
~ Psalm 121:2

Medical Journal

Date:

Change in Activity / Symptoms:

Concerns / Questions:

Medical Visit

Prayerful Warrior

☐ Follow up Required

☐ Hospital Stay Required

☐ Medication

New

Changed ☐ Removed ☐

Care Plans / Restrictions:

Problems / Adverse Effects:

Things to Watch / Special Instructions:

Prayer Journal

Lay Your Burdens at the Cross

Father in Heaven ...

The LORD bless you and keep you,
The LORD make His face shine upon you,
And be gracious to you,
~ Numbers 6:24-25

Medical Journal

Change in Activity / Symptoms:

Date:

Concerns / Questions:

Medical Visit

Prayerful Warrior

☐ Follow up Required

☐ Hospital Stay Required

☐ Medication

New

Changed ☐ Removed ☐

Care Plans / Restrictions:

Problems / Adverse Effects:

Things to Watch / Special Instructions:

Prayer Journal

Lay Your Burdens at the Cross

Father in Heaven ...

Be strong and of good courage, do not fear nor be afraid of them,
for the LORD your God, He is the One who goes with you.
He will not leave you nor forsake you.
~ Deuteronomy 31:6

Medical Journal

Change in Activity / Symptoms:

Date:

Concerns / Questions:

Medical Visit

Prayerful Warrior

☐ Follow up Required ☐ Hospital Stay Required ☐ Medication

New

Changed ☐ Removed ☐

Care Plans / Restrictions:

Problems / Adverse Effects:

Things to Watch / Special Instructions:

Prayer Journal

Lay Your Burdens at the Cross

Father in Heaven ...

Grace, mercy, and peace will be with you
from God the Father and from the Lord Jesus Christ,
the Son of the Father, in truth and love.

~ 2 John 1:3

Medical Journal

Change in Activity / Symptoms:

Date:

Concerns / Questions:

Medical Visit

Prayerful Warrior

☐ Follow up Required

☐ Hospital Stay Required

☐ Medication

New

Changed ☐ Removed ☐

Care Plans / Restrictions:

Problems / Adverse Effects:

Things to Watch / Special Instructions:

Prayer Journal

Lay Your Burdens at the Cross

Father in Heaven ...

I will praise You, for I am fearfully and wonderfully made,
Marvelous are Your works,
And that my soul knows very well.
~ Psalm 139:14

Medical Journal

Date:

Change in Activity / Symptoms:

Concerns / Questions:

Medical Visit

Prayerful Warrior

☐ Follow up Required ☐ Hospital Stay Required

☐ Medication

New

Changed ☐ Removed ☐

Care Plans / Restrictions:

Problems / Adverse Effects:

Things to Watch / Special Instructions:

Prayer Journal

Lay Your Burdens at the Cross

Father in Heaven ...

And do not lead us into temptation, But deliver us from the evil one.

For Yours is the kingdom and the power

and the glory forever. Amen.

~ Matthew 6:13

Medical Journal

Change in Activity / Symptoms:

Date:

Concerns / Questions:

Medical Visit

Prayerful Warrior

☐ Medication

☐ Follow up Required

☐ Hospital Stay Required

New

Changed ☐

Removed ☐

Care Plans / Restrictions:

Problems / Adverse Effects:

Things to Watch / Special Instructions:

Prayer Journal

Lay Your Burdens at the Cross

Father in Heaven ...

Praise the LORD!
Oh, give thanks to the LORD, for He is good!
For His mercy endures forever.
~ Psalm 106:1

Medical Journal

Date:

Change in Activity / Symptoms:

Concerns / Questions:

Medical Visit

Prayerful Warrior

☐ Follow up Required

☐ Hospital Stay Required

☐ Medication

New

Changed ☐ Removed ☐

Care Plans / Restrictions:

Problems / Adverse Effects:

Things to Watch / Special Instructions:

Prayer Journal

Lay Your Burdens at the Cross

Father in Heaven ...

The righteous cry out, and the LORD hears,
And delivers them out of all their troubles.

~ Psalm 34:17

Medical Journal

Change in Activity / Symptoms:

Date:

Concerns / Questions:

Medical Visit

Prayerful Warrior

☐ Medication

☐ Follow up Required

☐ Hospital Stay Required

New

Changed ☐ Removed ☐

Care Plans / Restrictions:

Problems / Adverse Effects:

Things to Watch / Special Instructions:

Prayer Journal

Lay Your Burdens at the Cross

Father in Heaven ...

Rejoice always, pray without ceasing, in everything give thanks,
for this is the will of God in Christ Jesus for you.

~ 1 Thessalonians 5:16 –18

Medical Journal

Change in Activity / Symptoms:

Date:

Concerns / Questions:

Medical Visit

Prayerful Warrior

☐ Medication

☐ Follow up Required

☐ Hospital Stay Required

New

Changed ☐ Removed ☐

Care Plans / Restrictions:

Problems / Adverse Effects:

Things to Watch / Special Instructions:

Prayer Journal

Lay Your Burdens at the Cross

Father in Heaven ...

The LORD is near to the brokenhearted
And saves those who are crushed in spirit.
~ Psalm 34:18 NASB

Medical Journal

Change in Activity / Symptoms:

Date:

Concerns / Questions:

Medical Visit

Prayerful Warrior

☐ Follow up Required ☐ Hospital Stay Required ☐ Medication

New

Changed ☐ Removed ☐

Care Plans / Restrictions:

Problems / Adverse Effects:

Things to Watch / Special Instructions:

Prayer Journal

Lay Your Burdens at the Cross

Father in Heaven ...

I can do all things through Christ who strengthens me.

~ Philippians 4:13

Medical Journal

Date:

Change in Activity / Symptoms:

Concerns / Questions:

Medical Visit

Prayerful Warrior

☐ Follow up Required

☐ Hospital Stay Required

☐ Medication

New

Changed ☐ Removed ☐

Care Plans / Restrictions:

Problems / Adverse Effects:

Things to Watch / Special Instructions:

Prayer Journal

Lay Your Burdens at the Cross

Father in Heaven ...

but we also glory in tribulations, knowing that tribulation
produces perseverance, and perseverance,
character, and character, hope.
~ Romans 5:3-4

Medical Journal

Change in Activity / Symptoms:

Date:

Concerns / Questions:

Medical Visit

Prayerful Warrior

- [ ] Medication

- [ ] Follow up Required
- [ ] Hospital Stay Required

New

Changed [ ] Removed [ ]

Care Plans / Restrictions:

Problems / Adverse Effects:

Things to Watch / Special Instructions:

Prayer Journal

Lay Your Burdens at the Cross

Father in Heaven ...

And those who know Your name will put their trust in You,
For You, LORD, have not forsaken those who seek You.
~ Psalm 9:10

Medical Journal

Date:

Change in Activity / Symptoms:

Concerns / Questions:

Medical Visit

Prayerful Warrior

☐ Medication

☐ Follow up Required

☐ Hospital Stay Required

New

Changed ☐ Removed ☐

Care Plans / Restrictions:

Problems / Adverse Effects:

Things to Watch / Special Instructions:

Prayer Journal

Lay Your Burdens at the Cross

Father in Heaven ...

What then shall we say to these things?
If God is for us, who can be against us?
~ Romans 8:31

Medical Journal

Date:

Change in Activity / Symptoms:

Concerns / Questions:

Medical Visit

Prayerful Warrior

☐ Follow up Required

☐ Hospital Stay Required

☐ Medication

New

Changed ☐ Removed ☐

Care Plans / Restrictions:

Problems / Adverse Effects:

Things to Watch / Special Instructions:

Prayer Journal

Lay Your Burdens at the Cross

Father in Heaven ...

A man's heart plans his way,
But the LORD directs his steps.
~ Proverbs 16:9

Medical Journal

Date:

Change in Activity / Symptoms:

Concerns / Questions:

Medical Visit

Prayerful Warrior

☐ Follow up Required

☐ Hospital Stay Required

☐ Medication

New

Changed ☐ Removed ☐

Care Plans / Restrictions:

Problems / Adverse Effects:

Things to Watch / Special Instructions:

Prayer Journal

Lay Your Burdens at the Cross

Father in Heaven ...

By this the love of God was revealed in us,
that God has sent His only Son into the world
so that we may live through Him.
~ 1 John 4:9 NASB

Medical Journal

Date:

Change in Activity / Symptoms:

Concerns / Questions:

Medical Visit

Prayerful Warrior

☐ Medication

New	
Changed ☐	Removed ☐

☐ Follow up Required

☐ Hospital Stay Required

Care Plans / Restrictions:

Problems / Adverse Effects:

Things to Watch / Special Instructions:

Prayer Journal

Lay Your Burdens at the Cross

Father in Heaven ...

He heals the brokenhearted

And binds up their wounds.

~ Psalm 147:3

Medical Journal

Date:

Change in Activity / Symptoms:

Concerns / Questions:

Medical Visit

Prayerful Warrior

☐ Medication

New	
Changed ☐	Removed ☐

☐ Follow up Required

☐ Hospital Stay Required

Care Plans / Restrictions:

Problems / Adverse Effects:

Things to Watch / Special Instructions:

Prayer Journal

Lay Your Burdens at the Cross

Father in Heaven ...

Draw near to God and He will draw near to you.

~ James 4:8

Medical Journal

Date:

Change in Activity / Symptoms:

Concerns / Questions:

Medical Visit

Prayerful Warrior

☐ Medication

New

Changed ☐ Removed ☐

☐ Follow up Required

☐ Hospital Stay Required

Care Plans / Restrictions:

Problems / Adverse Effects:

Things to Watch / Special Instructions:

Prayer Journal

Lay Your Burdens at the Cross

Father in Heaven ...

and the peace of God, which surpasses all understanding,
will guard your hearts and minds through Christ Jesus.
~ Philippians 4:7

Medical Journal

Date:

Change in Activity / Symptoms:

Concerns / Questions:

Medical Visit

Prayerful Warrior

☐ Medication

New

Changed ☐ Removed ☐

☐ Follow up Required ☐ Hospital Stay Required

Care Plans / Restrictions:

Problems / Adverse Effects:

Things to Watch / Special Instructions:

Prayer Journal

Lay Your Burdens at the Cross

Father in Heaven ...

Blessed is the man who trusts in the LORD,
And whose hope is the LORD.
~ Jeremiah 17:7

Medical Journal

Change in Activity / Symptoms:

Date:

Concerns / Questions:

Medical Visit

Prayerful Warrior

- [ ] Follow up Required
- [ ] Hospital Stay Required
- [ ] Medication

New

Changed [ ] Removed [ ]

Care Plans / Restrictions:

Problems / Adverse Effects:

Things to Watch / Special Instructions:

Prayer Journal

Lay Your Burdens at the Cross

Father in Heaven ...

Have I not commanded you? Be strong and of good courage,
do not be afraid, nor be dismayed, for the LORD
your God is with you wherever you go.
~ Joshua 1:9

Medical Journal

Change in Activity / Symptoms:

Date:

Concerns / Questions:

Medical Visit

Prayerful Warrior

☐ Medication

☐ Follow up Required

☐ Hospital Stay Required

New

Changed ☐ Removed ☐

Care Plans / Restrictions:

Problems / Adverse Effects:

Things to Watch / Special Instructions:

Prayer Journal

Lay Your Burdens at the Cross

Father in Heaven ...

But You, Lord, are a compassionate and gracious God,
Slow to anger and abundant in mercy and truth.
~ Psalm 86:15 NASB

Medical Journal

Date:

Change in Activity / Symptoms:

Concerns / Questions:

Medical Visit

Prayerful Warrior

☐ Medication

☐ Follow up Required

☐ Hospital Stay Required

New

Changed ☐ Removed ☐

Care Plans / Restrictions:

Problems / Adverse Effects:

Things to Watch / Special Instructions:

Prayer Journal

Lay Your Burdens at the Cross

Father in Heaven ...

But those who wait on the LORD shall renew their strength,
They shall mount up with wings like eagles, They shall run
and not be weary, They shall walk and not faint.
~ Isaiah 40:31

Medical Journal

Date:

Change in Activity / Symptoms:

Concerns / Questions:

Medical Visit

Prayerful Warrior

☐ Follow up Required

☐ Hospital Stay Required

☐ Medication

New

Changed ☐ Removed ☐

Care Plans / Restrictions:

Problems / Adverse Effects:

Things to Watch / Special Instructions:

Prayer Journal

Lay Your Burdens at the Cross

Father in Heaven ...

cast all your anxiety on Him, because He cares about you.

~ 1 Peter 5:7 (NASB)

Medical Journal

Date:

Change in Activity / Symptoms:

Concerns / Questions:

Medical Visit

Prayerful Warrior

☐ Follow up Required

☐ Hospital Stay Required

☐ Medication

New

Changed ☐ Removed ☐

Care Plans / Restrictions:

Problems / Adverse Effects:

Things to Watch / Special Instructions:

Prayer Journal

Lay Your Burdens at the Cross

Father in Heaven ...

And we know that all things work together for good to those who love God,
to those who are the called according to His purpose.
~ Romans 8:28

Medical Journal

Date:

Change in Activity / Symptoms:

Concerns / Questions:

Medical Visit

Prayerful Warrior

☐ Follow up Required

☐ Hospital Stay Required

☐ Medication

New

Changed ☐ Removed ☐

Care Plans / Restrictions:

Problems / Adverse Effects:

Things to Watch / Special Instructions:

Prayer Journal

Lay Your Burdens at the Cross

Father in Heaven ...

Jesus said to him, "If you can believe,
all things are possible to him who believes."
~ Mark 9:23

Medical Journal

Date:

Change in Activity / Symptoms:

Concerns / Questions:

Medical Visit

Prayerful Warrior

☐ Medication

New	
Changed ☐	Removed ☐

☐ Follow up Required

☐ Hospital Stay Required

Care Plans / Restrictions:

Problems / Adverse Effects:

Things to Watch / Special Instructions:

Prayer Journal

Lay Your Burdens at the Cross

Father in Heaven ...

Heal me, O LORD, and I shall be healed,

Save me, and I shall be saved,

For You are my praise.

~ Jeremiah 17:14

Medical Journal

Date:

Change in Activity / Symptoms:

Concerns / Questions:

Medical Visit

Prayerful Warrior

☐ Follow up Required

☐ Hospital Stay Required

☐ Medication

New

Changed ☐ Removed ☐

Care Plans / Restrictions:

Problems / Adverse Effects:

Things to Watch / Special Instructions:

Prayer Journal

Lay Your Burdens at the Cross

Father in Heaven ...

He who believes in Me, as the Scripture has said,
out of his heart will flow rivers of living water.
~ John 7:38

Medical Journal

Change in Activity / Symptoms:

Date:

Concerns / Questions:

Medical Visit

Prayerful Warrior

☐ Medication

New	
Changed ☐	Removed ☐

☐ Follow up Required

☐ Hospital Stay Required

Care Plans / Restrictions:

Problems / Adverse Effects:

Things to Watch / Special Instructions:

Prayer Journal

Lay Your Burdens at the Cross

Father in Heaven ...

For I, the LORD your God, will hold your right hand,
Saying to you, 'Fear not, I will help you.'
~ Isaiah 41:13

Medical Journal

Date:

Change in Activity / Symptoms:

Concerns / Questions:

Medical Visit

Prayerful Warrior

☐ Medication

New	
Changed ☐	Removed ☐

☐ Follow up Required

☐ Hospital Stay Required

Care Plans / Restrictions:

Problems / Adverse Effects:

Things to Watch / Special Instructions:

Prayer Journal

Lay Your Burdens at the Cross

Father in Heaven ...

Peace I leave with you, My peace I give to you,
not as the world gives do I give to you.
Let not your heart be troubled, neither let it be afraid.
~ John 14:27

Medical Tracker

Physician: *Date:*

Location/Facility:

Treatment:

Important Notes:

Physician: *Date:*

Location/Facility:

Treatment:

Important Notes:

Physician: *Date:*

Location/Facility:

Treatment:

Important Notes:

Physician: *Date:*

Location/Facility:

Treatment:

Important Notes:

Medical Tracker

Physician: *Date:*

Location/Facility:

Treatment:

Important Notes:

Physician: *Date:*

Location/Facility:

Treatment:

Important Notes:

Physician: *Date:*

Location/Facility:

Treatment:

Important Notes:

Physician: *Date:*

Location/Facility:

Treatment:

Important Notes:

Medical Tracker

Physician: *Date:*

Location/Facility:

Treatment:

Important Notes:

Physician: *Date:*

Location/Facility:

Treatment:

Important Notes:

Physician: *Date:*

Location/Facility:

Treatment:

Important Notes:

Physician: *Date:*

Location/Facility:

Treatment:

Important Notes:

Medical Tracker

Physician: *Date:*

Location/Facility:

Treatment:

Important Notes:

Physician: *Date:*

Location/Facility:

Treatment:

Important Notes:

Physician: *Date:*

Location/Facility:

Treatment:

Important Notes:

Physician: *Date:*

Location/Facility:

Treatment:

Important Notes:

Medical Tracker

Physician: *Date:*

Location/Facility:

Treatment:

Important Notes:

Physician: *Date:*

Location/Facility:

Treatment:

Important Notes:

Physician: *Date:*

Location/Facility:

Treatment:

Important Notes:

Physician: *Date:*

Location/Facility:

Treatment:

Important Notes:

Medical Tracker

Physician: *Date:*

Location/Facility:

Treatment:

Important Notes:

Physician: *Date:*

Location/Facility:

Treatment:

Important Notes:

Physician: *Date:*

Location/Facility:

Treatment:

Important Notes:

Physician: *Date:*

Location/Facility:

Treatment:

Important Notes:

Thank You!

Thank You for purchasing *Prayerful Warrior Mom Medical & Prayer Journal.*

I really appreciate all of your feedback and
I love hearing what you have to say.
I need your input to make the next version of this
journal and my future journals better.

Please take two minutes now to leave a helpful review on Amazon letting me know what you thought of the journal:

Thanks so much!

Tracy A Ripley

Other Journals in the Prayerful Warrior Mom Series

These journals were created to help you anchor your heart in faith, find strength in the storm, and walk this journey with hope and purpose.

Follow Tracy on social media and sign up for her mailing list at PrayerfulWarrior.com to stay updated on her latest releases, helpful resources, and to connect with a community of support.

More Titles by Tracy A. Ripley

Thank you so much for purchasing the *Prayerful Warrior Medical & Prayer Journal.* If you enjoyed using this practical resource, please check out *Prayerful Warrior Mom,* a transformative memoir written with raw honesty – a testament to the indomitable human spirit and the triumph of faith over fear.

Tracy A. Ripley is the award-winning author of *Prayerful Warrior Mom,* a Mom's Choice Awards® Gold Recipient, 2025 NYC Big Book Award WINNER in the category of Women's Health, Readers' Favorite Gold Medal Winner, and three-time First Place BookFest Award Winner. She lives in Ohio with her husband where she enjoys spending time with her children and grandchildren.

"...a roadmap for battling adversity and discovering inner strength." **~ The US Review of Books**

"This book is, indeed, a gift of faith to be shared." **~ The Book Commentary**

"Recommended to all parents of children with any major health challenge." **~ Readers' Favorite**

Made in United States
Cleveland, OH
22 October 2025

24308917R00080